Halloween

By MaryAnn McAlpin
Photos by Frank & Angela McAlpin

Halloween is coming!

Halloween is coming!

I have to get a costume.

I have to get a costume for Halloween.

What can I be?

What can I be for Halloween?

I can be a red candy.

I can be an orange pumpkin.

I can be a brown cat.

I can be a blue monster.

I like the brown cat.

I can be the brown cat for Halloween.

Happy Halloween!